It's Okay to Say No:
Choosing Sexual Abstinence

Many teens are choosing abstinence as an alternative to the risks of sexual activity.

The Teen Pregnancy Prevention Library

It's Okay to Say No:

Choosing Sexual Abstinence

by Eleanor Ayer

THE ROSEN PUBLISHING GROUP, INC.
NEW YORK

Published in 1997 by The Rosen Publishing Group, Inc.
29 East 21st Street, New York, NY 10010

First Edition

Library of Congress Cataloging-in-Publication Data

Ayer, Eleanor
    It's okay to say no: choosing sexual abstinence / by Eleanor
Ayer. — 1st ed.
       p.   cm. — (Teen pregnancy prevention library)
    Includes bibliographical references and index.
    Summary: Discusses what abstinence means, the dangers of teenage
sexual activity, the difficulty of choosing abstinence, and the
advantages of abstaining from sex.
    ISBN 0-8239-2250-2
    1. Sexual abstinence—Juvenile literature.   2. Teenagers—Sexual
behavior—Juvenile literature.   3. Birth control—Juvenile
literature.   4. Sexually transmitted diseases—Prevention—Juvenile
literature. [1. Sexual abstinence.   2. Youth—Sexual behavior.
3. Sexual ethics.]   I. Title. II. Series.
HQ27.A94   1997
306.73′2—dc20   96-35171
                                                    CIP
                                                       AC

Manufactured in the United States of America.

Contents

Abstinence is a smart choice when you don't feel ready to have sex.

1 What Abstinence Means

SAM AND SELENA HAD BEEN DATING FOR *three months. After their second date, Sam asked Selena if he could kiss her. With every date the kisses got more serious. Soon they were spending long hours in each other's arms. But when Sam asked Selena to have sex with him, she got scared.*

Before she started dating, Selena promised herself that she wouldn't have sexual intercourse until she was married. It had been easy to keep that promise until she met Sam. Now she wasn't so sure. She cared a lot about him. She thought that she might even love him. But she wasn't ready to have sex with him.

Selena believed in sexual abstinence. Abstinence, Selena thought, meant not doing certain physical things with someone because they could lead to trouble. But Selena was confused. Did "abstaining" mean just not having intercourse? Or did it also mean not even kissing? At what point should she slow down or stop her physical relationship with Sam?

Selena faced the same tough choices that many young people face when they begin serious dating. It's easy to promise yourself that you will be sexually abstinent when you are sitting alone in front of the television. But it's much harder when you are in the arms of someone you think you love. Can you love someone and still be abstinent?

The answer is yes. You should never have to "prove" that you love someone by having sex with them. You can still show someone that you love them by how you treat them, what you say, and the things you do.

The closer you get with someone physically, the harder it can be to remain abstinent. This book will help you to set limits and stick to them. Remember that what you want is just as important as what your boyfriend or girlfriend wants.

What Is Sexual Abstinence?

Abstinence means not partaking in something—for example, many people choose to abstain from drugs or alcohol. Sexual abstinence, to most people, means abstaining from sexual intercourse. It can also mean abstaining from other kinds of sexual activity. This book will help you to define abstinence in the way that is most appropriate for you.

The decision to be abstinent is a tough one, especially if you have already been sexually active.

It's Never Too Early (or Too Late) to Become Abstinent

Teens who have never been sexually active usually find it easier to abstain than those who have already been involved with someone physically. It is much easier to say "no" when you do begin to date if you commit yourself to abstinence beforehand.

But what if you are already sexually active? What if you've gone all the way with someone or come close to it? Is it too late for you to become abstinent? The answer is no—it's never too late. "Second virginity" is a term used when people who have once been sexually active want to practice abstinence. Several groups throughout the country support second virginity. They help teens who want to change their ways and practice abstinence, and they can answer your questions, too.

A growing number of young people realize that sex can have serious consequences. Teenagers who care about themselves don't want to risk disease. They also understand that having and raising a baby while they're still growing up themselves can be nearly impossible. For these teenagers, sexual abstinence is the answer.

Your Decision

This book will show you why abstinence can be a smart choice for you. It can be difficult to stick with a choice that is different from what your friends are doing. The number of teens who are sexually active continues to increase. Movies, advertising, television shows, and music videos often make having sex seem like a mature, adult thing to do. Teens who are sexually active are shown to be cool and popular. But just copying what you see doesn't make you cool. People are more impressed by the person who isn't afraid of standing apart from the crowd.

2 Abstinence as an Option

MOSES WAS FOURTEEN WHEN HIS SIXTEEN-
year-old sister Tiffany got pregnant. After the baby was
born, Tiffany lived at home with her family. She didn't
get married. In fact, she never saw the baby's father
again.

While she was pregnant, Tiffany was excited. She
wanted to have the baby. But after Toby was born,
Tiffany was grouchy all the time. She had a job, but
she didn't make much money. In order to work more
hours, she had to drop out of school. She rarely saw her
friends. Her life was a never-ending cycle of taking care
of the baby and going to work. The baby didn't seem
happy, either. He cried all the time.

The Problem of Teen Pregnancy

Tiffany is among the more than 1 million teenage
girls in the United States who get pregnant each
year. Most claim their pregnancies were "acci-
dents." Eighty-two percent of the girls say they
never expected to get pregnant. One out of every

One out of every five sexually active teenage girls becomes pregnant.

five teenage girls who are sexually active ends up getting pregnant.

Twenty years ago, the number of teen pregnancies was ninety-nine out of every 1,000 girls. Today that number is up to 120 per 1,000. By the age of eighteen, one out of every four American girls will have been pregnant at least once. That figure increases to nearly two out of four by the time girls reach twenty. Nearly one out of five teens who gets pregnant will be pregnant again within a year.

By getting pregnant at sixteen, Tiffany became one of the 40,000 teenage girls who drop out of school each year because they are pregnant. She became one of the teens who will earn only about half as much money in their lifetimes as women who start families in their twenties. Tiffany gets no money for child support. This makes her part of the 82 percent of unmarried mothers who receive no child support from their babies' fathers, even though fathers are legally required to pay child support.

Looking at Tiffany, Moses can't understand why any teenager would want a baby. His sister said once that if she could turn back the clock, she would not have had sex until she was married. Moses is very glad he is not in his sister's position. He doesn't have a child to support. He can go out with his friends and spend the money he makes on himself. He is still in school and plans to get a good education. After seeing what Tiffany's life is like, Moses has made himself a promise. He won't become sexually active until he's ready to get married. Then, if his wife became pregnant, they could help each other and be a family. But Moses knows he is not quite ready for all that responsibility yet.

Teenage Sexual Activity Is Increasing

Unfortunately, abstinence is not the sexual choice most teenagers make. Nearly one-third of all American fifteen-year-olds are sexually active. By the time they turn sixteen, half of all teenage boys have had intercourse. For black males, the age is even younger.

Sexual activity among teenagers is increasing steadily. In a recent six-year period, the percentage of fifteen- to nineteen-year-old girls who were sexually active rose from 42 percent to nearly 52 percent. By the time unmarried teens reach the age of twenty, 86 percent of males and 77 percent of females are sexually active.

Teenagers are not the only ones paying the price for this increase in sexual activity. It costs American taxpayers more than $30 billion a year to support families that are headed by unwed teenage mothers like Tiffany.

Why Is Teenage Sexual Activity on the Rise?

Many believe that television encourages greater sexual activity. By the time most young people graduate from high school, they have watched 15,000 hours of television, but only spent 12,000 hours in the classroom. A typical American teenager watches twenty-three hours of television a week. Children from low-income homes watch more than those from middle- or upper-income homes.

A typical one-hour TV program shows three sexual acts. The number is higher for daytime soap operas, which are watched by many teenage girls. A girl watching the soaps may see an average of 1,500 sexual acts per year. These scenes often suggest intercourse, prostitution, and rape.

On television, sexual activity between unmarried people happens six times more often than between married couples. This suggests that it is okay to have sex without being married. Television also sends messages about how teens should dress, wear their hair, talk, and act in order to appear cool and sexy. Commercials frequently use sex to interest consumers in their products.

It is important to realize that television focuses heavily on sex because it gets people's attention. TV producers want people to watch their shows, and advertisers want people to buy their products.

The typical teenager watches more than three hours of television a day, exposing him or her to many sex-related scenes and images.

They think that sex will sell their shows and products to the public. That's why television is full of sexual images—not because "everybody's doing it."

Saving Yourself for Marriage

The media, peer pressure, and today's lifestyles lure many teens to have sex even though they may not really want to. In a study done in Atlanta, Georgia, 90 percent of girls under sixteen who were questioned said they "wanted to learn how to 'say no' to sex."

Traditionally, many people waited to have sex until they were married. They were expected to "save themselves for marriage." Slowly, some of today's teens are going back to that idea. They are making a commitment to abstinence. They are promising themselves that they will not have sex before marriage—no matter how great the pressure becomes.

Becoming sexually involved can be a very emotionally stressful experience.

3 Dangers of Teenage Sexual Activity

"I'M ONLY FOURTEEN," SAYS ALEXA, "BUT I know some people who are already having sex. I think I'm too young and am probably going to be too young for a while. . . . It does have an emotional effect. You can be ready at fourteen physically, but mentally you might not be ready for a while."

The Dangers of Emotional Involvement

Alexa knows that the dangers of teenage sex are not just physical. During these years the body develops very rapidly. Hormones, chemicals released by the body's glands, cause body growth and development. Hormones also cause changes in the mind, including emotions. Mood swings—being positive and upbeat one day, sad and depressed the next—are common among most teenagers. Emotions can be very intense and unpredictable during the teenage years.

Because teenagers' moods and feelings are so changeable, this is not a good time to become emotionally involved. Just as teens like to try new hairstyles or a certain way of dressing, they also meet different kinds of people as they look for the right mate. "But when sex gets in the picture," says Yolanda, who's sixteen, "you're forced to make decisions that your mind is not ready to face." Being sexually involved means making choices that will affect you for the rest of your life.

Seventeen-year-old Michelle says she "was so in love with Brad after two dates that I was blind. I couldn't see that he didn't feel the same way about me. One night he asked me to go to his dad's hunting cabin out of town. I was very scared, but also very excited. I wouldn't have said 'no' for the world."

Looking back she says, "Having sex wasn't as wonderful as I had thought it would be." On the drive back to town Brad was quiet. Emotionally, Michelle was going crazy. "I felt guilt, pleasure, shame, love, fear—all mixed together. The next day Brad ignored me at school. After that he never called again. My world was shattered. Now I wish that night had never, ever happened."

The Dangers of Sexually Transmitted Diseases

Along with emotional problems, having sex can bring physical problems as well. Every year, 2.5 million teenagers are infected with some type of

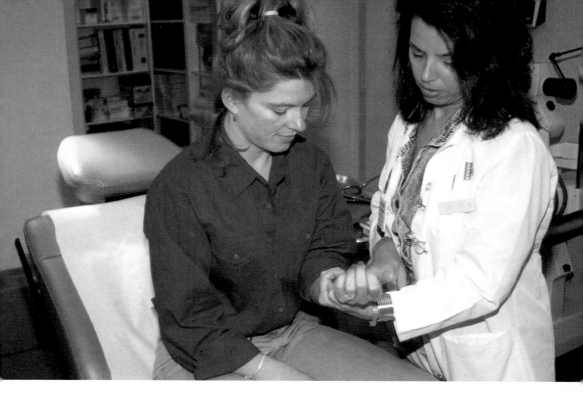

Sexual activity can expose you to many sexually transmitted diseases.

sexually transmitted disease (STD). Before the age of twenty-one, one out of every four teens will be affected.

AIDS, otherwise known as Acquired Immuno-deficiency Syndrome, has killed nearly one-quarter million Americans in the last decade. In 1992, AIDS was the leading cause of death among men twenty-five to forty-four. Many of them had contracted HIV, the virus that causes AIDS, as teenagers, but it takes the virus a number of years to kill its victims. One-quarter of all people who get the HIV virus are twenty-one or younger. At least one-third of all known AIDS cases are reported by people who have heterosexual (male/female) relationships.

AIDS is not the only sexually transmitted disease

that is a danger to teenagers. Gonorrhea, an inflammation of the genital organs, is one of the most common STDs. Syphilis is an infectious disease that can affect many parts of the body, but most often attacks the genitals. Like gonorrhea, it is passed along during intercourse. Extreme cases may cause death. Chlamydia, genital warts, and herpes are other common STDs.

Condoms offer some protection against STDs, but they are not 100-percent safe. Condoms can leak, break, or slip off. There is only one sure way for every person to protect against STDs— abstinence. Abstinence is by far the best protection against sexually transmitted diseases. That includes abstinence from any kind of sexual touching, because STDs can be passed on this way, too.

The Danger of Pregnancy

The United States has a higher rate of teen pregnancy than any other developed country in the world. Its rates of teenage birth and abortion are also the highest.

Sexually active teenagers who do not use birth control should expect to get pregnant. They should plan on it and decide what they will do. Will they choose abortion, adoption, or birth? Sexually active teens who assume that pregnancy will not happen to them are being immature and irresponsible.

Sexually active teens must be prepared to accept the risk that sex can lead to pregnancy and make them parents at a young age.

Missy was fifteen when she first became pregnant. She had been dating Jacob for several months. After school they would go to his house when no one was home. Missy knew from talking with friends that the danger of getting pregnant was very high when you didn't use protection—and she and Jacob sometimes got lazy about that. But she figured pregnancy would never happen to her. When it did, her parents had to pay for her to have an abortion.

Unfortunately, Missy did not learn from that experience. Within a year she was pregnant again by a different guy. This time her parents would not agree to an abortion. One month after she turned seventeen, Missy had her baby. Sadly, the baby was born with mental and physical disabilities caused by the father's use of drugs. The father disappeared. "I just wish I could tell other teens how stupid it is to have sex," says Missy. "I ruined my life, all for a few minutes of fun."

4 Abstinence: The Only Foolproof Birth Control

THERE IS ONE METHOD OF BIRTH CONTROL
that is 100-percent effective, guaranteed to work
every time. That method is abstinence: not having
sexual intercourse at all. Abstinence is the only
birth control that is absolutely safe. Not only does
it guard against pregnancy, it also protects against
sexually transmitted diseases.

Withdrawal Is Not a Form of Birth Control

*Zach and Mara had been dating for most of their
sophomore year. Many times they had "fooled around,"
but they had always stopped short of intercourse. Zach
wanted to try it. But Mara was afraid. She had
promised herself she would remain abstinent.*

*Zach loved Mara, but he also wanted to have sex.
He reminded Mara how far they had gone together. It
would be all right to go just a little farther and have
intercourse, if they stopped just before orgasm, he said.
That way there would be no danger of pregnancy, and
she would have kept her promise of abstinence.*

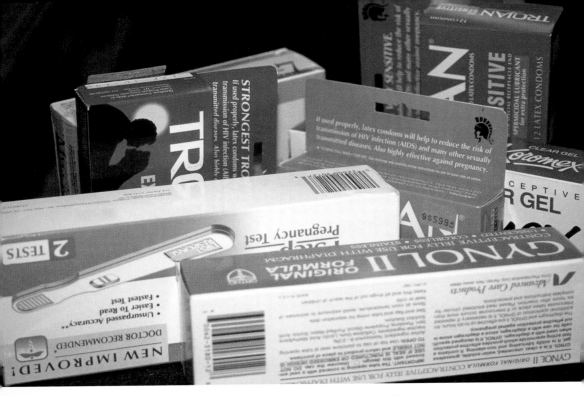

Abstinence is the only 100-percent effective method of birth control.

Zach was wrong in two ways. First, withdrawal is not a safe form of birth control. There is no way to predict the exact moment that sperm will enter the vagina during intercourse. Sperm can leak into the vagina before orgasm or before withdrawal. You can even get pregnant without having intercourse if sperm are near the vagina.

Second, people who use withdrawal are not practicing abstinence. Any sexual involvement—no matter how brief—means that you are no longer abstinent. In fact, many abstinent teens feel that any kind of intimate touching is a break from abstinence.

Failure Rates of Contraception

Sexually active teens must prepare themselves for pregnancy and for STDs. No contraceptive device can guarantee full protection. If you use no birth control and just trust your luck, the chances of getting pregnant are 85 percent, a very high risk. And even with birth control, there is still a risk.

The chart below shows you the chance of pregnancy with each kind of contraception. Remember, if you choose abstinence, the chance of pregnancy is zero percent!

METHOD	CHANCE OF PREGNANCY
Oral contraceptives (birth control pills)	3%
Diaphragm	2–23%
IUD (intrauterine device)	6%
Condom	12%
Withdrawal	18%
Rhythm (having intercourse only on those days of the month—relating to a woman's menstrual cycle—when conception is least likely)	20%
Foams	21%

Source: Zero Population Growth "Backgrounder"

The Abortion Option

Seventeen-year-old Connie never worried much about

birth control. She figured that if she got pregnant, she would just have an abortion. After all, she and Steve were both pro-choice. The idea of abortion did not bother her. She knew of a "no-questions-asked" clinic near her town. It all seemed quite simple.

What Connie did not know was how deeply pregnancy can affect a person's emotions. On the day she discovered she was pregnant, she got scared. Suddenly, the thought of abortion frightened her. She had to talk to someone. Things didn't seem as easy as they once had.

Connie called Steve. His reaction totally shocked her. "Connie, I want you to have our baby," he said. "And I want to get married." Connie was not ready to get married. She certainly was not ready to have a baby.

That weekend they talked. Steve told Connie he had never been against abortion before, but now that it was his child, he felt differently. When Connie told him she just couldn't go through with the pregnancy, Steve was hurt and angry. Even though they had both made a vow not to tell anyone, Steve told his parents. They agreed with Steve. They did not want Connie to have an abortion.

In the days after her argument with Steve, Connie started to see things in a different light. Her body was changing. Hormones were affecting her emotions in strange ways. She did not feel she could have a baby at that point in her life, but she wasn't so sure she wanted *an abortion either. She didn't know what she wanted to do. She felt alone, confused, and depressed.*

Abortion is a choice for people who cannot go through with the birth process for personal reasons. Many people who have had abortions agree: It may be the best option at the time, but the decision is never easy. You don't know exactly how you will feel until you are in that situation. It's better not to take the chance, and choose abstinence from the beginning. Abortion should never be considered a form of birth control.

Teenage sexual activity comes with very high risks and dangers. Teenagers who choose to be sexually active cannot ignore these warnings. There is no safe way for a teenager to have sex. The only totally safe choice is abstinence.

5 The Benefits of Abstinence

JENNIFER DID NOT CARE IF HER FRIENDS
called her a prude. She didn't argue with them. She
didn't preach to them. She didn't need to. She felt
comfortable with her decision. She was not going to
have sex until she was married.

It was not her parents or her religion that made
Jennifer choose abstinence. She wanted peace of mind.
She did not want the worry of getting sexually
involved. Jennifer knew what misery could come from
teenage sexual activity. Recently her sister Julie, who
was sleeping with more than one guy, had caught
gonorrhea.

When she first noticed soreness and redness around
her genitals, Julie thought she had a yeast infection.
Soon her bladder became inflamed. Sores developed
around her mouth. When pus started oozing from the
sores, Julie went to the doctor. To stop the infection from
spreading to her reproductive organs, the doctor pre-
scribed penicillin. She had to take large doses of it every
day and see the doctor often. Each time she visited he

checked her for signs of other diseases. Sometimes, he explained, gonorrhea covers up signs of syphilis, an STD that is harder to treat.

For months, Julie suffered pain and embarrassment. The medicine made her feel sick. She worried that she might have syphilis. Her parents were angry and the house was filled with tension. Watching her sister suffer was enough to convince Jennifer that she didn't want to have sex until she was married. Being a virgin was just fine.

No Risk of Pregnancy

Ivette had a different reason for deciding to be abstinent. Every day during her freshman year she passed a poster in the window of the school counselor's office. The picture on the poster showed a teenage mom holding a year-old baby. Underneath, the words read: IT'S LIKE BEING GROUNDED FOR EIGHTEEN YEARS. Ivette knew what it was like to be grounded for a month. Eighteen years would be like prison.

For most teenagers, having a baby is like being grounded. One or both parents must work to support the baby. This usually means that they do poorly in school or drop out altogether. When they are not working, they have to stay home and take care of the baby. If they do have a chance to go out, they must find and pay a babysitter or take the

Taking care of a baby is a twenty-four-hour-a-day job. To make ends meet, many teen moms must drop out of school and work long hours.

baby with them. As the child gets older, the problems get tougher and the costs get higher. There is no break from the many responsibilities of raising a child. Having a baby means having to take care of someone else, putting their needs and wants before your own.

Every hour in the United States alone, fifty-six babies are born to teenage mothers. The future for these children and their mothers is not very bright. Consider these statistics:

- Two-thirds of the families headed by teen mothers are poor.
- Half of all welfare payments go to families

headed by teenage mothers. And under new welfare laws, teen moms are not even guaranteed to receive welfare at all.

- Teen moms are twice as likely never to finish high school.
- Teen moms earn about half the income in a life-time that women who started families in their twenties earn.
- Teenage mothers are three times more likely to be separated or divorced. Some never marry at all.
- Daughters of teenage mothers tend to have children themselves as teenagers.

Being Honest with Your Family

Julio was an honest kid. Everyone trusted him. He liked it that way. It cut down on the stress in his life. He never had to worry about being caught in a lie. When he went out at night, his mom and stepdad knew he'd be back by curfew. They knew he would go where he said he was going, or call them if his plans changed.

When Julio went out with his girlfriend, his parents didn't worry. They knew Julio's feelings on sex. Long ago his mother had told him, "I don't ever want you to do to a girl what was done to me." Julio's mom was sixteen when he was born. On the day she told her boyfriend she was pregnant, he disappeared. She never saw him again. Her life had been very hard. She had

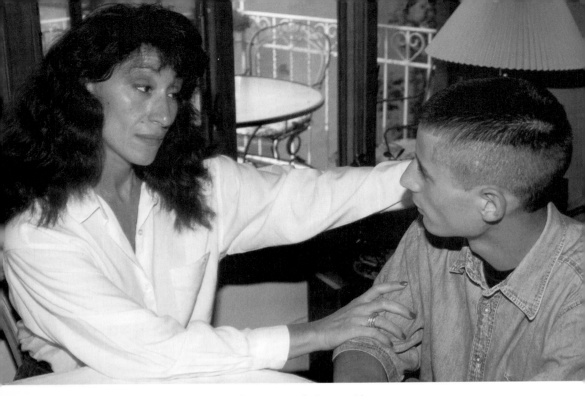

Abstinence can make it easier to be honest with your parents.

never been able to go to college like she had hoped. Until she married Julio's stepdad and was able to stay home with Julio, she always worked long hours for low pay.

Julio told his mother's story to his girlfriend, Liz. He also told her his feelings on abstinence, even though he felt a little strange. "It isn't you," he assured her. "It's me. It's something I have to do for myself." Liz seemed to understand. She respected Julio's feelings. "It's easier for me, too," she told him. "Not having to lie to my parents, or go behind their backs to get birth control, or worry about getting pregnant—that's a load off my mind. Abstinence makes it easier to be honest."

Knowing the Limits of Your Relationship

As the months went by, Liz found she liked abstinence more and more. Before Julio, her dates had often pressed her to have sex. When she said "no," they usually ended the relationship. At first that had bothered her. Dating was important in her life.

But after she started dating Julio, Liz saw things differently. She felt comfortable, knew where they stood with each other, and she felt she could trust him. At the end of the evening, he wasn't going to try to get her into bed. He also would not threaten to end their relationship if she didn't sleep with him.

Can Abstinence Make the Heart Grow Fonder?

There is an old saying: "Absence makes the heart grow fonder." It means that being away from someone can make that person love you, and you love them, even more. Can the same be said about abstinence? Will not having sex with a person make the person like you better? Will you care more for them? Often the answer is yes. Two people may be more attracted to each other if they have saved that special part of their relationship for later.

Patrick and Karen had been dating for about two months. After a movie or a night with friends, they would sit in the car, talking and kissing. One night Patrick asked Karen if she would sleep with him.

In her heart, Karen wanted to sleep with Patrick. She felt great when she was with him. It would be harder to say no to Patrick than to any other boy she had dated. But long ago she had promised herself that she would stay abstinent until she was married.

Still, she was worried. If she said no to Patrick, would it anger him? Would it end their relationship? The thought scared her, but she stayed firm. Abstinence meant a great deal to her. She intended to stick by her decision.

With difficulty, she explained this to Patrick. She was prepared for his frustration and disgust. Instead Patrick kissed her. "You're so different from other girls I've gone out with," he said. "You really know what you want. I like that about you. And I can deal with not having sex."

6 The Difficulty of Abstinence

J. J. FELT OUT OF IT. EVERY TIME HIS BASKETBALL *team played out of town, they spent the entire bus ride talking about their sexual experiences. J. J. was almost seventeen and he had never had sex. He'd had plenty of dates, but he'd never gone out with the same girl more than twice. He liked it that way. He didn't have to worry about physical or emotional involvement.*

Tonight his team members seemed to be after him. "Let's hear about it, J. J. Tell us about Marlena. Is she good? What did you do?" When he didn't answer, somebody said, "Forget about J. J. He's a card-carrying virgin."

J. J. wanted to crawl under his seat. Even his last date had asked him, "J. J., is it true what I hear about you? Are you really a virgin?" When J. J. said yes, she looked shocked, then laughed. "Wow, I can't believe it! I thought there were no virgins left at this school!"

Fear of Rejection
At such times, J. J. hated himself for being abstinent. He wondered if he'd made the wrong

Pressure and teasing from your friends can make it difficult to be abstinent.

choice. Many teens in J. J.'s position wonder the same thing. It's easy to decide on abstinence when you're home alone or when you're listening to a teacher in a sex education program. But it's not so easy when you're out on a date or under pressure from friends.

Teens often worry that sexual abstinence will make them unpopular. Never having had sex can make them feel naive and inexperienced. When everyone else is talking about their sexual adventures, it can be embarrassing to not know what these are like firsthand. Feeling left out can lower a person's self-esteem. It's hard to be called a virgin or prude by your classmates.

Peer pressure is one of the biggest reasons for teen sexual activity. A recent poll done for the Planned Parenthood Federation asked 1,000 teenagers why they did not wait until they were older to have sex. One-third of the girls and almost the same number of boys blamed peer pressure. Like J. J., they couldn't take being teased by fellow students for being abstinent. Almost as many girls said they had sex because boys put pressure on them. Nearly as large a group said they were sexually active because "everyone does it." They worried about being rejected by friends and fellow students. The fear of being different or standing out from the crowd was simply too great.

Saying "No" to a Persistent Partner

Another reason why teens—especially girls—may find it difficult to be abstinent is that they may feel pressured by their boyfriends or girlfriends. In the Planned Parenthood survey, 17 percent of the girls said that boys put pressure on them to have sex. But only 2 percent of the boys felt that they pressured girls. And there was no record of boys feeling pressured by girls to have sex. What does this mean? Are boys pressuring girls and just not admitting it?

The truth is that we still live in a society where, in most cases, boys are expected to make the first move in a sexual relationship. Boys are expected to be persistent. Girls are expected to say "no." Until there is a change in that attitude, girls will continue to feel more pressured than boys.

What is needed, says professor and psychologist Thomas Lickona, is mutual respect. "Love is wanting what is best for the other person, now and in the future," he says. "Teens need to know that if someone pushes for sex by saying, 'If you loved me, you would,' they can truthfully reply: 'If *you* loved *me*, you wouldn't ask.'"

Gina Soule of the Clallam Jefferson Family Planning Center in Port Angeles, Washington, has written a brochure for teens titled "Knowing How to Say No." In it, she offers three suggestions for being successful at abstinence:

- *Know your feelings*. Ask yourself some tough questions about your morals and values, so you know for certain where you stand.
- *Expect respect*. Recognize that different people have different opinions, but be confident about your own. State your feelings clearly and firmly. Don't feel that you must get defensive or argue about your choice of abstinence.
- *Be in control*. Don't allow yourself to get into troublesome situations, such as dating a person who is known to be sexually active. Don't let

Your decision to be abstinent should be respected by the people you date.

drugs or alcohol affect your judgment. Keep calm and stay away from risky situations. Make certain that you are the one in charge.

The Pain of Saying "No" When You'd Rather Say "Yes"

Eunice Kennedy Shriver, sister of the late U.S. President John F. Kennedy, works closely with teenagers. She tells of going to a teen center for girls "where the teacher asked what they would like to discuss most." The girls showed little interest in topics like family planning or child care. Then the teacher asked, "'Would you like to discuss how to say "no" to your boyfriend without losing his love?' All hands shot up."

Learning how to say "no" when you really want to say "yes" is one of the hardest parts of abstinence. Sixteen-year-old Sarah knew this very well. Sarah wasn't being pressured by her boyfriend to be sexually active, nor was she getting pressure from her friends. It was Sarah herself who wanted to have sex.

Three years earlier she had told herself she would not have intercourse until she was married—no matter what. But now she found herself wanting to be physically close to Jake. It was very hard for her to overlook this desire. When they talked about it, Jake confessed that he had wanted to make love for a long time, but he was trying to respect Sarah's pledge of abstinence.

"If we give in to our feelings," Jake reminded her, "we might regret it for the rest of our lives. You know if we do it once, we'll do it again. After the first time, it'll be easy." Sarah thought about it. She knew what she wanted to do. She also knew what she should do. It was a terribly hard choice, but in the end they both said "no" to having sex.

The decision brought Jake and Sarah closer together. They found it was sort of exciting, imagining what it would be like to make love with each other someday. They knew that if they gave in to their feelings now, the excitement and anticipation would be over.

There was another comforting thought. Jake and Sarah knew that if they did not marry each other, they would have no feelings of guilt or regret later for having lost their virginity to each other.

Breaking up with someone is often even more painful if you have been sexually active with them.

7 Why Abstinence Is Worth the Trouble

"I WOULD DO ANYTHING, *ANYTHING*," SAYS A man who was a sexually active teenager, "to forget the sexual experiences I had before I met my wife." Even though he has been married for eight years, he cannot forget those teenage years. "When I'm with my wife, the pictures of the past and the other women go through my head, and it kills any intimacy."

A young woman who has had sex with many partners feels the same way. She regrets her past and wishes she could do it over again—much differently. "That sick, used feeling of having given a precious part of myself—my soul—to so many, and for nothing, still aches. I never imagined I'd pay so dearly and for so long."

In the Long Run

The pain of having been a sexually active teen can last a lifetime. It can affect any teenager who is sexually active, not just those who get a disease or find themselves pregnant. Over the years, psychologist Dick Purnell has heard from many patients who wish they had been abstinent. "They say, 'At first it [sex] was very, very exciting. Then I started to feel bad about the person I was with. We started to argue and fight a lot. Then we broke up, and now we're enemies.'"

The pain after breaking up can be bad for both sides. Says one sixteen-year-old, "I get upset when I see my friends losing their virginity to some guy they've just met. Later, after the guy's dumped them, they come to me and say, 'I wish I hadn't done it.'"

Why does breaking up with a sexual partner cause people such pain? Psychologist Purnell offers an answer. "When you share your body with someone," he says, "you're giving part of yourself. When that someone leaves your life, something of you goes with him or her. You'll never get it back."

A Word from Teenage Parents

When Jackson and Sophia became parents, he was seventeen and she was eighteen. Right away, they got married. Today, after eighteen years of marriage, the couple says they don't have regrets. "But if I could do one thing differently," says Jackson, "I wouldn't have had sex as a teenager. Kids having sex is nothing but risky business—and not just when the girl gets pregnant. Of course, you couldn't have told me that then.

Many teen parents warn other teens not to make the same mistakes they did.

People tried, but I didn't listen. I just knew nothing was going to happen to me."

"We coped," says Sophia, "but coping is a lot different than planning your life in advance and making it go the way you want."

With his own kids, Jackson is very strict. He does not want them making the same mistake. "I tell my kids to trust me on this one. Maybe they won't listen to me on all things. But when it comes to having sex as a teenager, I've been there, I've done it, and it's no good."

A Word from Abstinent Teens

Teenagers who choose abstinence rarely have regrets. Those who are sexually active very often have regrets, ranging from broken hearts to destroyed lives. "Nobody's ever died from not having sex," says Kathleen Sullivan, director of Project Respect, an abstinence-based sex education program. Abstinence is risk-free. But sexually active teens are at high risk, both physically and emotionally.

"Love is like a step ladder," says Camille, a student at University High School in Los Angeles. "You start low, with the first step, and continue on to the higher steps. . . . If you start in the middle or at the top, as a lot of young people try to do [by having sex], you quickly fall down."

Scott, another student, believes that friendship and love must come first in a relationship. Begin, he says, by dating a friend, someone you respect and whose companionship you enjoy. Scott did just that. As their relationship grew, he discovered that "I loved her so much that I didn't want to have sex with her."

How do abstinent teens handle peer pressure to be sexually active? How do they keep their friends and keep their values at the same time? "You have to have faith in yourself," says sixteen-year-old Ling. "You have to be convinced that abstinence is best. When you act like you're not sure, it's easy for people to break you down, to talk you out of it. But when you show them that you can't be broken, that you're not going to change, they figure, 'Okay, that's cool.' Of course your friends—if they're real friends—wouldn't try to change you anyway."

A Word from Some Big Names

"We're all sexual," says TV and film actor Ted Danson. "But there are lots of ways to show someone you love them without having sexual intercourse." Ted stars in a video for teenagers entitled *How Can I Tell if I'm Really in Love?* "Sex is never a test of love, never," Danson reminds teens in the film. "Don't let anybody, no matter who, talk you into doing something you don't feel right about doing."

TV and film actress Justine Bateman co-hosts the film. "If the guy or girl says they'll leave you if you won't sleep with them," she warns teens, "they're probably not in love with you. This is the kind of person that's going to leave you right after you sleep with them anyway."

Dr. Sol Gordon, an expert on family and sex education, also appears in the film. "Of the ten most important things in a relationship," counsels Dr. Gordon, speaking to a large group of high school students, "sex is number nine." When students asked him what was first on the list, he named trust, caring, and friendship. Second was a sense of humor, and third was good communication.

Gordon warns his audiences, "Love can go from near perfect one day to a disaster the next. . . . Even committed relationships are spoiled by premature sex."

Choosing abstinence is not easy, but it has many rewards. It allows you to take charge of your own body and protect yourself from pregnancy, disease, and emotional pain. The next chapter will explain how to take the step of being abstinent.

8 Making Sexual Abstinence Work for You

A STRONG SENSE OF SELF-CONFIDENCE IS ONE of the keys to making sexual abstinence work.

The Importance of Self-Confidence

Whenever people take a stand that is different from what most people think, they must have strong confidence in themselves and faith in their decision. There are many pressures to act or think like everyone else. Without a strong sense of self-confidence, it is very hard to fight those pressures.

Seventeen-year-old Yaminah, who lives in Washington, DC, is proud to be a virgin. She says, "I'm not scared to tell boys I'm a virgin. It's better to be a virgin because boys have more respect for you, and you don't have to worry about AIDS tests and pregnancy tests or anything."

Today, Yaminah is proud of the fact that she's different from the majority. She is proud of the self-confidence she has developed. "Sometimes boys say there are no more virgins in Washington,

DC. I don't want to be classified like everybody else. Not everybody is like the girls on the videos wearing that little skimpy stuff."

Teens who have made a commitment to abstinence must be firm with themselves. They must have faith in their decision, even when they are feeling a lot of pressure. Chad, who is sixteen, is dating Crystal, a seventeen-year-old girl from his high school. Together they help support each other's decision to be abstinent. When they go out on dates, "if we start kissing, usually we both stop each other," Chad says. "We know what it can lead to."

Many teens have found that it helps to speak their opinions out loud. Getting into a discussion about abstinence with other teens can be a great confidence builder. It can give kids the strength to say "no" to a partner. Fourteen-year-old Raj discovered this when he and eighteen-year-old Quentin were talking. "It isn't cool for a boy to tell a girl no," said Quentin.

"Why isn't it?" asked Raj.

"You would tell a girl no?" asked Quentin, surprised.

"Yeah," said Raj, "because you might not be ready, and you don't want to take the responsibility. You might catch AIDS or other STDs, or get the girl pregnant." Hearing himself speak this way to

It is easier to stay abstinent when you go out with people who share your commitment to abstinence.

Quentin helped Raj become much more self-confident. He was proud of himself for having the courage to stand up to an eighteen-year-old. He no longer felt self-conscious or embarrassed about being abstinent.

Don't Lead Yourself into Temptation

In the film *Sex and Decisions: Remember Tomorrow*, two teenagers find themselves alone for the day at a beach house. There they are faced with the question of whether or not to have sex. They wrestle with temptation and discuss why they decided to act as they did. By going to the beach house, the pair put themselves into a situation that invited a problem. The temptation to have sex was very great. It took tremendous willpower for either one to say "no."

One of the best ways to remain abstinent is to avoid temptation. It can be as simple as agreeing to date only in a group. Teens who do not allow themselves to get into tempting situations find it much easier to say "no" to sex. One thing is certain: there will probably be no "slips" from abstinence if there are no temptations to have sex.

A good way for abstinent teens to avoid temptation is to date people who know their views and respect them. Seventeen-year-old Jorge was proud of the change in himself. "I told Mariana the first time we went out that I wasn't the same person she had known two months before. I told her that when my brother Pablo went to jail, I cleaned up my act. I don't do drugs anymore and I don't have sex. She knew me when I was a wild man, so I thought she probably wouldn't want to go out with the 'new' me. But hey, we're having a great time." Jorge's old girlfriend wanted nothing to do with him after his change. But that didn't bother him. "I know I'm right this time," he says confidently. "If she doesn't like the new me, that's just tough. I don't want to see her, either."

It can help to talk with friends who have also decided to be abstinent.

Strength in Numbers

Tina was watching the news one night when she saw a segment on a group of students in another city who had started an abstinence program at their school. Tina knew from talking to her friends and classmates that a lot of kids in her school were tired of hearing that all that teenagers thought about was sex. A lot of people she knew were either already abstinent, or thinking about becoming abstinent. She could think of a dozen people who would probably become members of an abstinence group. "I'm going to start a group, too," Tina had decided by the time the segment was over.

She started by asking her health teacher, Mr. Robinson, to be the group adviser. He agreed, and gave her some pamphlets about STDs, AIDS, and teen pregnancy. Tina took some of the information from the pamphlets and used it on her poster advertising her new group. Under a list of facts, she wrote: "These are all good reasons NOT to have sex right now. . . . Come to a meeting of an abstinence support group to talk to others who have decided to wait."

Ten people showed up for the first meeting—a pretty good turnout, Tina thought. And the meetings grew after that, as people heard from their friends that the group was a good place to talk about how they felt pressured to have sex. In the spring, Mr. Robinson asked Tina to talk to a school assembly about abstinence. When she graduated, the principal, Mrs. Cuevas, gave her a special award for her work.

If your school does not already have an abstinence program or support group, you can talk to a teacher, principal, or counselor about starting one. Contact one of the organizations at the back of this book for information on starting a program at your school. Check also to see if there is a program or group at your church or synagogue. Programs and support groups can help to provide encouragement to students who want to be abstinent.

Teens who feel alone in their decision to be abstinent can find support through groups and programs that focus on abstinence. It helps to talk with other teens who are facing similar issues.

Many schools offer abstinence-based or abstinence-only sex education programs. Among the more widely used programs is Teen Aid, which centers on teenage health problems that can result from being sexually active. Another program, Values and Choices, stresses the importance of honesty, respect, responsibility, promise-keeping, self-control, justice, and equality. Sex Respect focuses on teen sexuality and talks about issues such as dating and peer pressure.

Some teens who have made a commitment to sexual abstinence take a vow in front of others. Taking a vow seems to make their promise to themselves stronger. Part of their vow is to be firm with themselves when the pressure to have sex becomes great. Being firm means being able to say no under any circumstances.

Members of a nationwide teen abstinence group called True Love Waits sign pledge cards. Some girls wear chastity pledge rings that show they are virgins. Members like fifteen-year-old Lyndi say the rings help "if you're on a date or something. You know how guys sometimes want to go too far. You just look down at your ring, and it's a very visual reminder to wait . . . you think, I don't want to do this."

Glossary

abortion The medical procedure for ending a pregnancy, usually within the first three months.

AIDS Acquired Immunodeficiency Syndrome. A sexually transmitted disease that attacks the body's immune system and is carried by the HIV virus. AIDS is always fatal.

birth control Various methods used to make pregnancy less likely.

climax (orgasm) The peak of sexual arousal. It is usually marked by the ejaculation of sperm in men and vaginal contractions in women. (Sperm can leak out of the penis before or after ejaculation, however.)

commitment A promise to stay devoted in a relationship.

emotions Strong feelings.

genitals Sexual organs.

gonorrhea A sexually transmitted disease that produces an inflammation of the genital organs.

heterosexual Sexual orientation toward members of the opposite sex.

hormones Chemicals made by certain glands in the body that help a person grow and stay healthy.

intimacy Very close emotional or physical contact.

penis The male sexual organ.

pro-choice Favoring a woman's right to make her own decision on the issue of abortion.

second virginity The return to sexual abstinence after having been sexually active.

sexual abstinence To do without or refrain from having sexual intercourse or sexual contact.

sexual intercourse Sexual contact in which the penis enters the vagina.

sexually transmitted disease (STD) A disease, such as AIDS, that is transmitted through sexual contact with another person.

sperm Male fertilizing fluid.

syphilis A sexually transmitted disease that causes serious health problems.

vagina The female sexual organ.

virgin A person who has never had sexual intercourse.

withdrawal A usually ineffective method of birth control where the penis is removed from the vagina just before climax.

Help List

Advocates for Youth
1025 Vermont Avenue, NW
Suite 200
Washington, DC 20005
(202) 347-5700

Athletes for Abstinence
A. C. Green Programs for Youth
P.O. Box 17283
Los Angeles, CA 90017
(800) AC-YOUTH

The Best Friends Foundation
2000 N Street, NW
Washington, DC 20036
(202) 822-9266

Boys and Girls Clubs of America
1230 West Peachtree Street
Atlanta, GA 30309-3447
(404) 815-5700
Web site: http://www.proxima.com:8080/n_assembly/
 html/mem_bgca.html

Girls, Inc.
National Research Center
441 West Michigan Street
Indianapolis, IN 46202

(317) 634-7546
e-mail: hn3580@handsnet.org

Planned Parenthood Federation of America, Inc.
810 Seventh Avenue
New York, NY 10019
(212) 261-4300
e-mail: communications@ppfa.org
Web site: http://www.ppfa.org/ppfa

SIECUS: Sexuality Information and Education
     Council of the United States
130 West 42nd Street
New York, NY 10026
(212) 819-9770
Web site: http://www.siecus.org

True Love Waits
c/o Sunday School Board of the Southern Baptist
     Convention
127 Ninth Avenue North
Nashville, TN 37234-0152
(800) LUV-WAIT
e-mail: 70423.3230@compuserve.com

In Canada:

Planned Parenthood Federation of Canada
1 Nicholas Street, Suite 430
Ottawa, Ontario K1N 7B7
(613) 241-4474

For Further Reading

Bode, Janet. *Kids Having Kids: People Talk About Teen Pregnancy*. New York: Franklin Watts, 1992.

Fenwick, Elizabeth, and Richard Walker. *How Sex Works*. New York: Dorling Kindersley Publishing, 1994.

Kuklin, Susan. *What Do I Do Now: Talking About Teenage Pregnancy*. New York: G. P. Putnam's Sons, 1991.

Lauersen, Niels H., and Eileen Stukane. *You're in Charge: A Teenage Girl's Guide to Sex and Her Body*. New York: Fawcett Columbine, 1993.

Madaras, Lynda. *My Body, My Self*. New York: Newmarket Press, 1995.

Moe, Barbara. *Everything You Need to Know About Sexual Abstinence*. New York: Rosen Publishing Group, 1996.

Reynolds, Marilyn. *Detour for Emmy*. Buena Park, CA: Morning Glory Press, 1994.

Rozakis, Laurie. *Teen Pregnancy: Why Are Kids Having Babies?* New York: Twenty-First Century Books, 1993.

Video

How Can I Tell if I'm Really in Love? Paramount Pictures, 1986.

Index

About the Author

Eleanor Ayer has written many books for children and young adults on social issues, history, and biography. She holds a master's degree in literacy journalism from Syracuse University. Ms. Ayer lives in Colorado.

Photo Credits

Cover by Ira Fox; p. 41 by Lauren Piperno; p. 47 by Yung-Hee Chia. All other photos by Ira Fox.

Layout and Design

Erin McKenna